INVESTIGATING PHONICS

VOWEL SOUNDS

Written by
Kevin Rigg

Published by
World Teachers Press®

Teacher's Notes

The activities found on each sheet follow a familiar format. Once the students are familiar with the format, more teaching emphasis can be placed upon the sound being covered at that time. There will be less time needed explaining answer formats to the students.

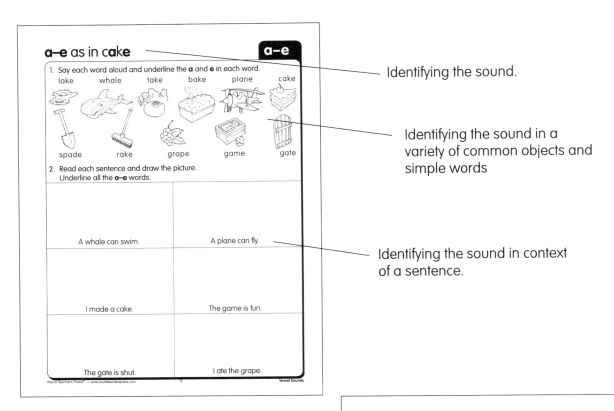

Identifying the sound.

Identifying the sound in a variety of common objects and simple words

Identifying the sound in context of a sentence.

Applying the sound to words and placing the word in context within a sentence.

Identifying and using the word in a range of fun and creative activities.

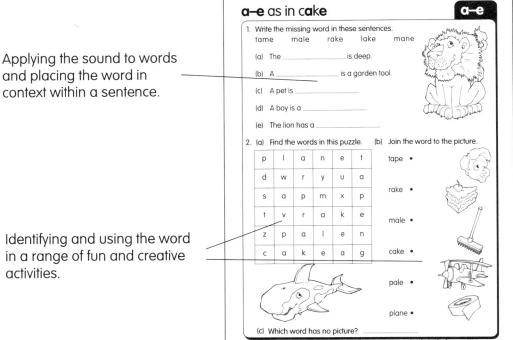

Activity Overview

Vowel Sounds		Identifying sounds in words	Adding missing sounds	Speaking words aloud	Unjumbling words	Cover and write words	Copying words	Cloze reading	Joining sentences	Selecting correct words	Read and draw	Yes/no answers	Matching words and pictures	Matching words and clues	Word searches
a–e	cake	✔		✔				✔			✔		✔		✔
ai	train	✔		✔			✔	✔	✔			✔	✔		
ey	obey	✔	✔	✔	✔	✔		✔	✔		✔				✔
ay	tray		✔	✔	✔	✔		✔			✔				✔
e	me	✔	✔	✔							✔			✔	
ea	leaf	✔	✔	✔				✔			✔		✔		✔
ee	tree	✔	✔	✔		✔	✔			✔		✔			✔
ey	key	✔	✔	✔	✔	✔		✔				✔			✔
ie	thief	✔	✔	✔	✔	✔			✔		✔	✔			✔
y	funny	✔		✔	✔	✔		✔	✔		✔	✔		✔	
i	blind	✔	✔	✔		✔		✔			✔	✔			✔
i–e	kite	✔	✔		✔	✔		✔		✔	✔				
y	sky	✔		✔							✔		✔		
o	cargo	✔	✔	✔		✔			✔		✔	✔			✔
oa	boat	✔	✔	✔	✔	✔					✔	✔			✔
o–e	bone	✔		✔	✔	✔		✔			✔		✔		✔
ow	show	✔	✔	✔		✔			✔	✔	✔			✔	
ew	stew	✔	✔	✔	✔	✔			✔		✔				✔
oo	spoon	✔		✔		✔		✔		✔	✔	✔			✔
u–e	flute	✔	✔	✔	✔	✔			✔	✔	✔			✔	

Record Sheet

Class:		a–e cake	ai train	ey obey	ay tray	e me	ea leaf	ee tree	ey key	ie thief	y funny	i blinds	i–e kite	y sky	o cargo	oa boat	o–e bone	ow show	ew stew	oo spoon	u–e flute
Room:																					
Teacher:																					

Word List

The following words are those found in the phonics worksheets for use in review or extension work.

a-e	ai	ey	ay	e	ea	ee	ey	ie	y
tame	train	they	may	he	teach	bee	donkey	thief	funny
male	first aid	whey	tray	me	beach	tree	trolley	shield	bunny
rake	sail	prey	day	we	read	feed	monkey	believe	dizzy
lake	pail	hey	today	she	beak	sleep	parsley	grief	jelly
mane	rain	survey	lay	be	eat	sheep	chimney	relief	granny
tape	snail	obey	hay	even	leaf	creek	key	piece	happy
cake	mail		pay	evening	speak	seed	valley	brief	puppy
pale	tail		stay		leap	peel	turkey	field	hurry
plane	nail		play		meat	deed	jockey	chief	sorry
whale	brain		ray		clean	green	honey		silly
game			bay		beat	feet			cherry
grape			crayon		seat	seek			valley
spade			gray		bean	peep			
gate					eagle	jeep			
take					tea				
made					dream				
ate					neat				
bake									

i	i-e	y	o	oa	o-e	ow	ew	oo	u-e
blinds	like	dry	pony	toad	home	grown	stew	spoon	rude
tiger	bike	cry	both	soap	slope	show	new	roof	rules
Friday	hive	sky	clover	boat	rode	crow	grew	boot	tune
behind	five	fry	total	goat	rose	yellow	jewel	food	flute
idea	hide	sty	post	coat	hose	hollow	crew	moon	pollute
kind	drive	my	cargo	loaf	hope	shadow	chew	broom	cute
spider	time	by	open	coach	bone	low	few	room	tube
iron	bite	why	most	moan	alone	burrow	threw	moo	use
find	fine	shy	over	foam	nose	slow	blew	balloon	cube
	nice	fly		roast	cone	below	brew	soon	mule
	kite			toast	poke	grow		groom	prune
	line			load	rope	narrow			June
	fire			float	stone	slowly			
	alive			road	stove				
	Mike				note				
	dive								
	live								
	mice								
	rice								
	hike								
	spike								
	dive								

Vowel Sounds We Need to Know

o   ey   ea   ai   ay

ee   a–e   ay   oa   y

u–e   ow   ew   i–e   ie

oa   o–e   e   i   y

Fill in the missing sounds.

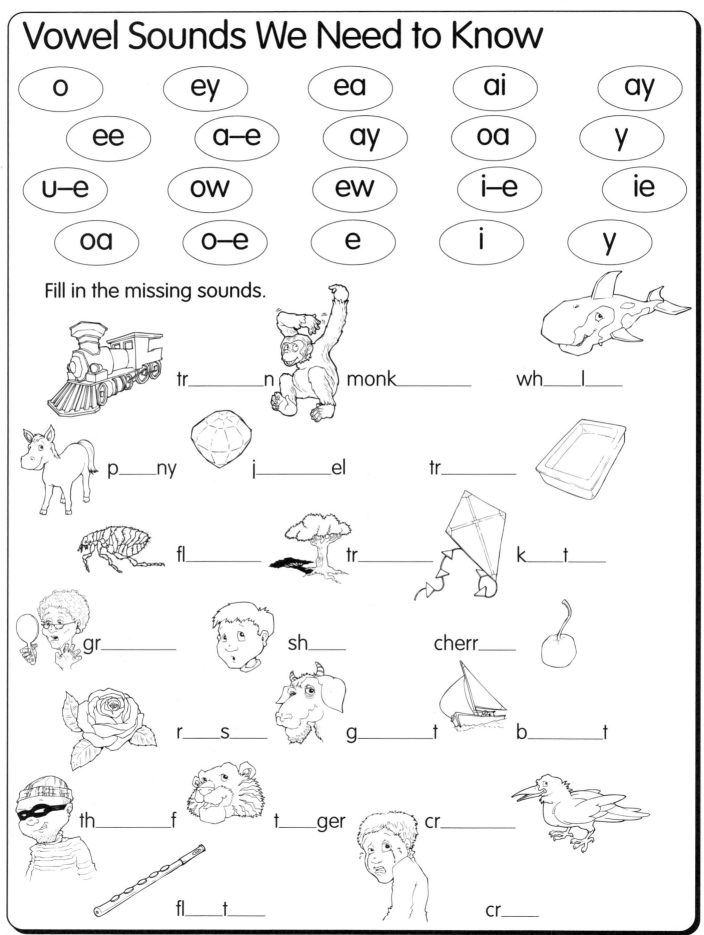

tr_____n   monk_____   wh____l__

p____ny   j_____el   tr_____

fl_____   tr_____   k____t____

gr_____   sh____   cherr____

r____s____   g____t____   b____t

th_____f   t____ger   cr_____

fl____t____   cr____

a–e as in cke

1. Say each word aloud and underline the **a** and **e** in each word.

| lake | whale | take | bake | plane | cake |

| spade | rake | grape | game | gate |

2. Read each sentence and draw the picture.
   Underline all the **a–e** words.

A whale can swim.	A plane can fly.
I made a cake.	The game is fun.
The gate is shut.	I ate the grape.

a–e as in cake

1. Write the missing word in these sentences.

   tame   male   rake   lake   mane

   (a) The _____ is deep.

   (b) A _____ is a garden tool.

   (c) A pet is _____.

   (d) A boy is a _____.

   (e) The lion has a _____.

2. (a) Find the words in this puzzle.

p	l	a	n	e	t
d	w	r	y	u	a
s	a	p	m	x	p
t	v	r	a	k	e
z	p	a	l	e	n
c	a	k	e	a	g

   (b) Join the word to the picture.

   tape   •

   rake   •

   male   •

   cake   •

   pale   •

   plane •

   (c) Which word has no picture? _____

ai as in train

1. (a) Read the words. Draw a line under the **ai** sound.

train

first aid

snail

rain

pail

mail

nail

sail

tail

   (b) Copy all the **ai** words here.

2. Write the missing **ai** word.

   (a) I stepped on the cat's _____.

   (b) When I _____ on the river,

   I take my _____ _____ kit.

   (c) I got the _____ at the post office.

   (d) I got wet because I was out in the _____.

   (e) I saw a _____ crawling.

   I put it in a _____.

   (f) A _____ is made of metal and is sharp.

ai as in train

1. Answer yes or no.

   (a) Can a train fly? _____

   (b) Does a snail have a tail? _____

   (c) Is a pail made of rock? _____

   (d) Can a snail do first aid? _____

   (e) Can you sail in the rain? _____

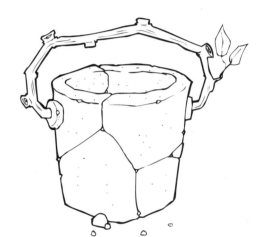

2. Write the correct word next to the picture.

   snail   rain   sail   pail   brain   tail   mail   nail   train

 _____    _____

 _____    _____

 _____

 _____   _____

3. Join these to make sentences.

   (a) The sailboat   •   • is very furry.

   (b) A cat's tail   •   • sailed on the lake.

   (c) Snails come out   •   • in the nail pail.

   (d) I put the nails   •   • on train tracks.

   (e) A train goes   •   • when it rains.

ey as in ob**ey**

1. Read the words aloud and underline the **ey** sound.

whey   they   prey   hey

survey   obey

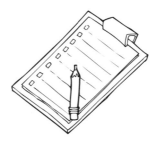

2. Read the sentence and choose the correct word.

whey   prey   they   obey

(a) The tiger will _____ upon other animals.

(b) Little Miss Muffet was eating curds and _____.

(c) Dad asked me to _____ him.

(d) When it rained _____ all got wet.

3. Unjumble these **ey** words.

(a) rpye _____

(b) vreuys _____

(c) heyt _____

(d) ybeo _____

(e) eyh _____

4. Read and draw.

Little Miss Muffet ate her whey.	The rabbit was prey for the fox.

ey as in obey

1. Match the sentence beginnings with the correct endings.

   (a) A cute bunny   •   • curds and whey.

   (b) Miss Muffet ate   •   • is prey to a fox.

2. Find all the words in the puzzle.
   Check them off as you find them.

   ☐ survey

   ☐ prey

   ☐ whey

   ☐ hey

   ☐ obey

   ☐ they

			h	e	y			
		g	r	h	y	b		
	r	s	u	r	v	e	y	
o	b	e	y	t	h	e	y	h
	e	p	h	p	r	e	y	
		w	h	e	y	a		
			u	e	r			

3. Add the **ey** sound to these words.
   Say each word as you make it.

   h_____   ob_____   surv_____

        wh_____   th_____   pr_____

4. Cover the worksheet and see how many **ey** words you can remember.
   Write them here.

   _____

   _____

   _____

   _____

ay as in tray

1. Use the letters in the stars to make **ay** words.

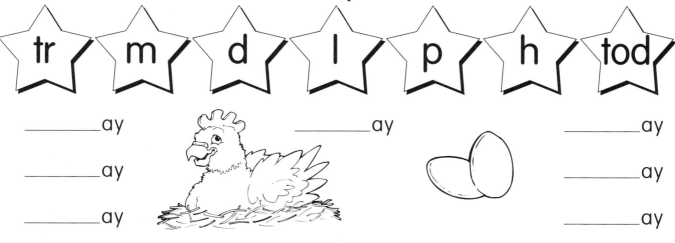

tr   m   d   l   p   h   tod

_____ay

_____ay

_____ay

_____ay

_____ay

_____ay

2. Read the sentence and choose the correct word.

(a) We went for a walk _____.

(b) The farmer cut the _____.

(c) I _____ with my friends.

(d) Did you _____ in the motel?

(e) A hen can _____ an egg.

stay
lay
play
hay
today

3. Read and draw.

Mother asked me to play outside.	The sun's rays shine.	I watched the little red hen lay an egg in the hay.

ay as in tray

1. Find these words in the puzzle.

   tray   say   stay   play   hay

   may   crayon   pay   today   bay

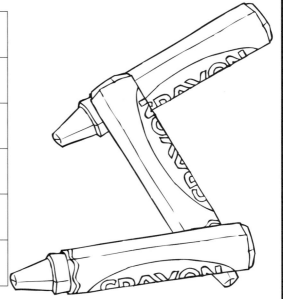

t	o	d	a	y	m	l	c
r	b	a	y	s	a	y	r
a	m	u	p	a	y	g	a
y	a	p	l	a	y	z	y
s	e	h	a	y	x	s	o
s	t	a	y	u	h	f	n

2. Unjumble these **ay** words.

   (a) yap _____

   (b) dtyoa _____

   (c) yha _____

   (d) yrnoac _____

   (e) ytas _____

   (f) aby _____

   (g) yrat _____

   (h) aym _____

3. Add the **ay** sound to these words. Say each word as you make it.

   st_____   tod_____   pl_____   tr_____   s_____

4. Cover the **ay** words. Write as many as you can without looking.

   _____

   _____

   _____

e as in me

1. Say each word aloud as you underline the **e** sound.

he   we   be   she

me   even   evening

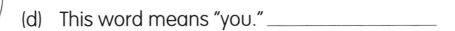

2. Write the word that matches the clue.

(a) The boy word.   _____

(b) The girl word.   _____

(c) All of us.   _____

(d) This word means "you." _____

(e) At night.   _____

3. Add the **e** sound to these.

___vening   m___   b___   h___

sh___   ___ven   w___

4. Read and draw.

We are looking at a black cat. She is even looking at me.	"Good evening," said Dad. He had a funny hat on. He even had a coat on.

ea as in leaf

1. Say these words aloud and circle the **ea** sound.

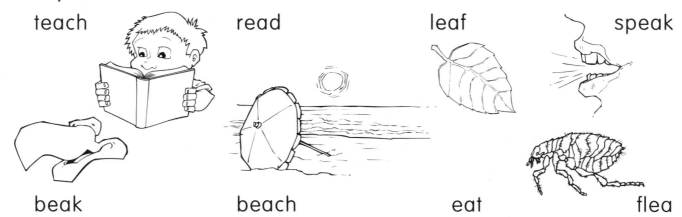

teach   read   leaf   speak

beak   beach   eat   flea

2. Fill in the missing **ea** sound.

t_____ch   b_____k

fl_____   cl_____n

sp_____k   t_____

b_____t   m_____t

r_____d

3. Draw a line from the word to the picture.

seat

beak

meat

read

4. Read the sentence and choose the correct word.

eat   leaf   beach   neat   meat   clean

(a) We had a swim at the _____.

(b) I must _____ my room and make it

_____.

(c) I can _____ my _____ with a fork.

(d) The _____ fell off the tree.

ea as in leaf

1. Find all the **ea** words in this word search.

neat
teach
clean
dream
bean
leaf
beat
beach

r	t	e	a	c	h	m	u
n	l	e	p	l	e	a	f
e	d	e	b	e	a	c	h
a	d	r	e	a	m	w	h
t	b	e	a	n	n	f	l
t	v	m	t	n	c	l	v

2. Match the words that rhyme.

(a) teach •   • clean

(b) bean •   • beach

(c) beat •   • seat

3. Read and draw.

The eagle will eat the fat flea with his clean beak.	We ate the beans at the beach.

ee as in tree

1. Read the words. Draw a line under the **ee** sound.

peel    bee    seed    feed

sleep   tree   sheep   creek

2. Color the correct word.
   Choose one sentence and draw a picture.

   (a) I | feed | seed | my cat.

   (b) The | deed | tree | is tall and | green | sheep | .

   (c) My | sleep | feet | got wet in the | seek | creek | .

   (d) The | sheep | bee | have wool on them.

   (e) A | feed | bee | has a stinger.

3. Finish the **ee** words.

   sh_____p   sl_____p   p_____p

   tr_____   f_____t   b_____

4. Copy the eight **ee** words from this sheet. Write them here.

   _____

   _____

ee as in tree

1. Find the **ee** words in this puzzle.

seed   sleep

seek   tree

bee   deed

creek   feet

peel   jeep

d	k	c	r	e	e	k	s
e	j	e	e	p	e	e	l
e	f	e	e	t	r	e	e
d	r	s	e	e	k	a	e
w	b	e	e	t	u	d	p
o	x	u	s	e	e	d	t

2. Cover the word puzzle and see how many **ee** words you can remember. Write them here.

_____

_____

_____

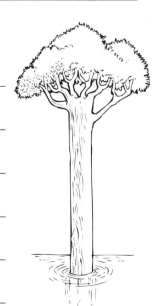

3. Answer yes or no.

(a) Can a bee sit in a tree?   _____

(b) Does a jeep sleep?   _____

(c) Have sheep got green feet?   _____

(d) Can you feed on a seed?   _____

(e) Can a creek do a good deed?   _____

(f) Can a tree grow in a creek?   _____

ey as in key

1. Read the words aloud and underline the **ey** sound.

donkey   trolley   chimney   monkey   parsley

key   valley   turkey   jockey   honey

2. Write the missing word in these sentences.

honey	jockey	turkey	trolley	monkey

(a) The poor _____ fell off his horse in the race.

(b) A _____ is used to move heavy things.

(c) We all had _____ on warm toast for breakfast.

(d) A big black _____ sat on the tree branch at the zoo.

(e) I had to feed the _____.

3. Unjumble these letters to make **ey** words.

(a) yek   _____   (b) kryeut   _____

(c) kdnoey   _____   (d) eonhy   _____

(e) nkomye   _____   (f) sareply   _____

(g) levaly   _____   (h) yockje   _____

4. Cover the sheet and see how many **ey** words you can write here.

_____

_____

ey as in key

1. Answer yes or no.

(a) Can a monkey sit on a chimney? _____

(b) Will a valley talk to a turkey? _____

(c) Can a donkey use a key? _____

(d) Is honey sweet? _____

(e) Does a turkey have a tail? _____

(f) Can parsley push a trolley? _____

2. Find all the words in the puzzle.

chimney   monkey

donkey   parsley

honey   trolley

valley   jockey

c	h	i	m	n	e	y	l
j	o	o	o	a	e	n	v
o	n	b	n	v	k	d	a
c	e	k	k	a	e	o	l
k	y	e	e	v	k	n	l
e	o	y	y	a	e	k	e
y	p	a	r	s	l	e	y
t	r	o	l	l	e	y	l

3. Finish the **ey** words.

monk_____   hon_____   jock_____   parsl_____

turk_____   vall_____   chimn_____   troll_____

ie as in thief

1. Read these words aloud and circle the **ie** sound.

thief   shield   believe   grief

brief   relief   piece   chief   field

2. Join the sentence beginning to its correct ending.

(a) The thief stole   •   • set up camp in the field.

(b) The team showed grief   •   • for supper last night.

(c) The chief   •   • for their stolen shield.

(d) We had a piece of cake   •   • it will rain tomorrow.

(e) I believe that   •   • the team's shield.

3. Write the missing **ie** sound in these words.

th_____f   br_____f   p_____ce   gr_____f

ch_____f   f_____ld   sh_____ld

4. Read and draw.

The thief had the old shield in his hand.	The chief ate a piece of cherry pie.	The girl showed grief when she fell in the field.

ie as in thief

1. Answer yes or no.

   (a) Can a chief carry a shield? _____

   (b) Can a field eat a piece of apple? _____

   (c) Does a crying boy show grief? _____

   (d) Do you believe we need food to live? _____

   (e) Can a rock show relief? _____

2. Find all of the **ie** words in the word search.
   Cross off the words as you find them.

believe	b	e	l	i	e	v	e	e	t	field
chief	r	e	l	r	e	l	i	e	f	piece
shield	c	h	i	e	f	i	e	l	d	relief
	t	s	h	i	e	l	d	k	e	
	t	v	r	a	p	i	e	c	e	

3. Unjumble these **ie** words.

   (a) ehift _____   (b) lhdesi _____

   (c) eeicp _____   (d) lerfie _____

4. Cover the sheet and see how many **ie** words you can remember. Write them here.

   _____

   _____

y as in funny

1. Say each word aloud and circle the **y** sound.

funny   happy   silly   granny   sorry

bunny   dizzy   jelly   puppy   hurry   cherry

2. Read the sentence and choose the correct word.

bunny	funny	puppy	jelly	sorry	silly	granny

(a) The clown was very _____ and he did some

   _____ things.

(b) My _____ runs after my pet _____.

(c) We all had _____ and ice cream for dessert.

(d) I told my _____ that I was very _____
   for missing her birthday.

3. Answer yes or no.

(a) A bunny can be silly.   _____

(b) Granny can make jelly.   _____

(c) A puppy can sit on a sorry.   _____

(d) I can eat a dizzy.   _____

(e) A cherry can be in the jelly.   _____

(f) The puppy can be very happy.   _____

y as in funny

1. Join the sentence beginning with the correct ending.

   (a) Mother put a red cherry   •   • then he ran after my bunny.

   (b) My granny was so sorry   •   • in the jelly.

   (c) The puppy ate his dinner   •   • that she made me hurry.

   (d) When I was sick I felt dizzy •   • live in the green valley.

   (e) Lots of very happy people •   • and my red face felt funny.

2. Read and draw.
   The silly bunny looked
   funny when it got dizzy.

3. Unjumble these **y** words.

   (a) pahpy   _____

   (b) nyufn   _____

   (c) lejyl   _____

   (d) ppyup   _____

   (e) ruhry   _____

   (f) zyidz   _____

4. Find the **y** word which matches the clue.

   (a) Makes you laugh.   ____ ____n____ ____

   (b) A grandparent.   g____ ____ ____ ____ ____

   (c) To feel good.   ____ ____ ____p____

   (d) A furry pet.   ____ ____n____ ____

   (e) This can be eaten.   ____h____ ____ ____ ____

i as in blinds

1. Say each word aloud and underline the **i** sound.

   blinds   Friday   idea   kind   find

   behind   tiger   spider   iron

2. Read the sentence and choose the correct word.

tiger	behind	Friday	spider	blinds	find	iron	kind

   (a) It is _____ of Mother to _____ my clothes.

   (b) The kitchen _____ will be fixed on _____.

   (c) You can _____ a _____ at the zoo.

   (d) _____ the chair was a little _____ in its web.

3. Answer yes or no.

   (a) A tiger can fly to the moon. _____

   (b) We use an iron to drive a car. _____

   (c) We go to school on Friday. _____

   (d) A pig can hide behind a spider. _____

   (e) Blinds are used on windows. _____

   (f) A spider is a kind of animal. _____

4. Cover the sheet and see how many **i** words you write here.

   _____

   _____

i as in blinds

1. Add the missing **i** sound to these words. Draw a picture to show the meaning of the word.

t___ger	___ron	beh___nd	sp___der
bl___nds	k___nd	___dea	f___nd

2. Find the words in the puzzle. Check the words off as you find them.

blinds   iron

Friday   idea

kind   spider

find   behind

tiger

F	r	i	d	a	y	m	f
b	e	h	i	n	d	w	o
w	f	u	i	r	o	n	g
r	s	p	i	d	e	r	i
t	i	g	e	r	m	k	k
r	u	f	i	n	d	i	i
h	b	l	i	n	d	s	n
c	h	m	j	f	e	d	d

i-e as in kite

1. Underline the **i** and **e** in these words.

five   line   hide   drives   time   bite   fine

2. Choose the correct word. Write it in each sentence.

   (a)   Jill has _____ dollars.

   (b)   Today is a _____ sunny day.

   (c)   Mr. Brown _____ a red car.

   (d)   You can draw a _____ with a ruler.

   (e)   I had a _____ of the chocolate bar.

   (f)   It is _____ for lunch.

   (g)   Let's play _____ and seek.

3. Color the correct word in each sentence.

   (a)   The man | bites | drives | a big green truck.

   (b)   My | kite | kitten | can fly high in the sky.

   (c)   I had a | bite | hide | of the apple.

   (d)   I wear a watch to tell the | line | time |.

   (e)   You should never play with | fire | alive |.

4. Read and draw.

Five bees flew near the hive.	I pulled my kite as I rode my bike.	The man went for a hike in the forest.

i–e as in kite

1. Add **ike** to make new words.

like

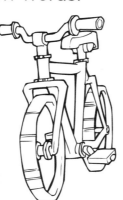

b_____ ____ ____

h_____ ____ ____

M_____ ____ ____

sp_____ ____ ____ ____

2. Add **ive** to make new words.

alive

d_____ ____ ____

f_____ ____ ____

h_____ ____ ____

l _____ ____ ____

3. Choose the correct word. Write it in the space below.

(bike)   (hive)   (rice)   (mice)   (line)

(a) The _____ have very long tails.

(b) Draw a _____ on the page.

(c) I can ride a _____.

(d) I love to eat _____.

(e) Bees live in a _____.

4. Unjumble these **i–e** words.

(a) tiek _____ ____ ____ ____

(b) iemc _____ ____ ____ ____

(c) iehk _____ ____ ____ ____

(d) ikel _____ ____ ____ ____

(e) vife _____ ____ ____ ____

(f) kbei _____ ____ ____ ____

5. Cover the page and see how many **i–e** words you can write here.

_____

_____

y as in sky

1. Say each word and underline the **y** sound.

dry   fry   my   why   cry

sky   sty   by   shy   fly

2. Write the correct word to match the picture.

(a) _____

(b) _____

(c) _____

(d) _____

(e) _____

(f) _____

(g) _____

(h) _____

3. Read and draw.

When a plane goes by it is flying in the sky.	The pig sty was too dry.	The fly on my arm began to cry.

4. Cover the page and see how many **y** words you can write here.

_____

_____

_____

o as in cargo

1. Say each word to yourself and circle the **o** sound in each word.

pony	clover	post	cargo	both

total	open	most	over

2. Join the sentence beginnings with the correct ending.

   (a) A pony ate • • of fence posts.

   (b) Both of the boys • • most of the clover.

   (c) The boat had a cargo • • the pony will get away.

   (d) If the gate is open • • got over the fence.

3. Read and draw.

The pony walked over the clover.	Both birds had their beaks open.	The boat had a cargo of fence posts.

4. Cover the page and see how many **o** words you can write here.

_____

_____

_____

o as in cargo

1. Answer yes or no.

   (a) A pony can eat a post. _____

   (b) A post is part of a fence. _____

   (c) Most people have over ten fingers. _____

   (d) A boat can have a cargo of clover. _____

   (e) The total of 2 and 4 is 6. _____

2. Add the missing **o** sound to these words.

   carg____   p____ny   t____tal   cl____ver

   ____ver   ____pen   m____st   p____st   b____th

3. Find the **o** words in the word search. Check off the words as you find them.

   total   over

   both   open

   cargo   most

   clover   post

   pony

	p	o	v	e	r	
u	c	t	o	t	a	l
b	l	c	a	r	g	o
o	o	b	p	o	n	y
t	v	o	m	o	s	t
h	e	p	o	s	t	m
	r	o	p	e	n	

oa as in boat

1. Say these words. Circle the **oa** sound.

loaf   load   goat   boat   float

foam   toad   coat   soap   toast   moan

2. Answer yes or no.

   (a)   A toad can jump over a leaf.   _____

   (b)   A goat wears a coat in the sea.   _____

   (c)   A football coach can moan.   _____

   (d)   The soap will foam if you rub it. _____

   (e)   The boat has a long tail.   _____

3. Finish these words by adding the **oa** sound.

   c_____ch   b_____t   r_____st   t_____d

   c_____t   s_____p   t_____st   r_____d

4. Draw pictures for three **oa** words.

oa as in boat

1. Unjumble these **oa** words.

    (a) toca _____   (b) falot _____

    (c) aops _____   (d) gaot _____

    (e) mofa _____   (f) aotd _____

    (g) falo _____   (h) adlo _____

    (i) sotta _____

2. Find the **oa** words in the word puzzle.

goat   load

foam   toad

float   loaf

coat   boat

toast   soap

i	k	g	o	a	t	h	z
j	l	o	a	f	o	a	m
k	z	l	l	o	a	d	s
b	o	a	t	g	s	n	o
b	f	l	o	a	t	m	a
c	o	a	t	o	a	d	p

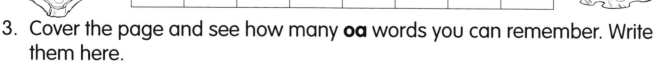

3. Cover the page and see how many **oa** words you can remember. Write them here.

_____

_____

_____

o–e as in bone

1. Say the word and underline the **o–e** letters.

home  slope  bone rode

rose hose hope alone

2. Read and draw.

The dog has a bone.	Mother saw the rose.
Tim rode to the moon.	This is my home.

3. Choose the correct word. Write it in the space below.

rose	home	slope	bone	nose

(a) Mother grew a _____ in the garden.

(b) My dog likes to chew a _____.

(c) My _____ has a roof.

(d) The bike went down the _____.

(e) My _____ is on my face.

o–e as in bone

1. Join the **o–e** word to the picture.

hose
home
bone
rose
cone
stove

2. Find these words in this puzzle.

note   slope   poke

stone   rope   bone   nose

t	s	t	o	n	e
b	l	v	g	o	r
o	o	d	k	t	o
n	p	o	k	e	p
e	e	n	o	s	e

3. Unjumble these **o–e** words.

(a) ncoe   _____

(b) meoh   _____

(c) ntose   _____

(d) ekpo   _____

(e) oben   _____

(f) lespo   _____

4. Cover the page and see how many **o–e** words you can write here.

_____

_____

_____

ow as in show

1. Say each word and underline the **ow** sound.

grown   yellow   slow   burrow   shadow

below   crow   hollow   low   show   grow

2. Join the sentence beginnings with the correct ending.

(a)	The big black crow	•	•	below the ground.
(b)	The hollow in the tree	•	•	moving very slowly.
(c)	I saw a snail in the garden	•	•	had a yellow beak.
(d)	A rabbit lives in a burrow	•	•	to make my shadow grow.
(e)	I will show you how	•	•	was very narrow.

3. Fill in the missing **ow** sound in these words and draw a picture to show its meaning.

shad_____	holl_____	yell_____
burr_____	cr_____	sl_____

ow as in show

1. Color the correct words.

   (a) When the sun shines I have a
   | shadow | narrow | .

   (b) The pretty bird was | slowly | yellow | and lived in a
   | hollow | below | tree.

   (c) A rabbit will quickly hop into its
   | burrow | shadow | .

   (d) The door was too | narrow | yellow | for the fat dog.

   (e) A tree will | show | grow | very | slowly | crow | in
   winter.

2. Write the **ow** word that matches the clue.

   (a) Nothing inside.   h___ ___ ___ ___ ___

   (b) Not very fast.   s___ ___ ___

   (c) Underneath.   ___ ___l___ ___

   (d) Not very wide.   n___ ___ ___ ___

   (e) To get bigger.   ___r___ ___

   (f) A black bird.   ___r___ ___

3. Cover the page and see how many **ow** words you can write here.

   _____

   _____

   _____

ew as in st**ew**

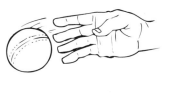

1. Say each word as you draw a circle around the **ew** sound.

blew  crew  jewel  chew

grew   new   stew   threw   few

2. Unjumble these **ew** words.

(a) eblw   _____

(b) tesw   _____

(c) wcer   _____

(d) gewr   _____

(e) rweht   _____

(f) wen   _____

(g) eelwj   _____

(h) wehc   _____

3. Read and draw.

The man threw the corn in the stew.	Mother has a new jewel.

4. Finish these words by adding the **ew** sound.

thr_____   j_____el   n_____   ch_____   gr_____

f_____   bl_____   cr_____   st_____

ew as in st**ew**

1. Find the **ew** words in the puzzle.

   blew   brew

   jewel   threw

   chew   new

   crew   stew

   few   grew

			j	s	y			
		z	e	t	w	i		
	x	g	w	e	f	m	n	
t	h	r	e	w	c	h	e	w
t	t	e	l	b	r	e	w	v
n	y	w	f	h	e	d	x	j
	b	l	e	w	w	p	b	
		d	w	r	c	d		
		q	d	c				

2. Join the correct endings to make sentences.

   (a) The ship's crew   •   • she got new shoes.

   (b) The wind blew   •   • in a new bag.

   (c) When her feet grew   •   • had a stew for dinner.

   (d) The thief threw the jewel •   • a few leaves off the tree.

3. Cover the sheet and see how many **ew** words you write here.

   _____

   _____

   _____

oo as in spoon

1. **Read the words. Circle the oo sound.**

spoon  moon  broom

roof boot food room

2. **Choose the correct word.**

(a) We use a _____ to sweep the floor.

(b) A cow goes _____.

(c) I eat my ice cream with a _____.

(d) The _____ shines in the sky at night.

(e) On a cold day we wear our _____.

boots
moon
broom
spoon
moo

3. **Read and draw.**

I eat my food with a spoon.	The old boot was on the roof.	The broom was in the room.

4. **Cover the page and see how many oo words you can write here.**

_____

_____

        Investigating Phonics – Vowel Sounds

oo as in spoon

1. Answer yes or no.

    (a) We can eat food in a room.   _____

    (b) I can put a spoon on the moon.   _____

    (c) A boot can go moo.   _____

    (d) A balloon can go on the roof.   _____

    (e) I can use a broom.   _____

2. Find the **oo** words in the puzzle.

spoon   soon

roof   moon

groom   food

broom   boot

balloon

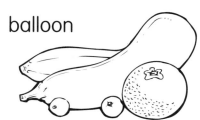

l	b	a	l	l	o	o	n
s	p	o	o	n	g	a	s
b	o	o	t	f	r	w	o
i	q	d	m	o	o	n	o
o	s	b	r	o	o	m	n
r	o	o	f	d	m	v	l

3. Write the correct **oo** word to match the picture.

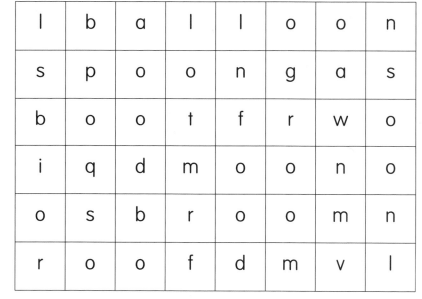

(a) _____   (b) _____

(c) _____   (d) _____

u–e as in flute

1. As you say each word, underline the **u** and **e**.

   rude   pollute   cute   use   rules

   tune   flute   tube   cube

2. Color the correct word. Select one sentence and draw its picture.

   (a)   The lady played a ⬚tune⬚ ⬚cute⬚
         on her ⬚cube⬚ ⬚flute⬚.

   (b)   I ⬚use⬚ ⬚tune⬚ a ⬚tube⬚ ⬚mule⬚ of
         toothpaste.

   (c)   The ⬚prune⬚ ⬚rude⬚ child threw a
         ⬚prune⬚ ⬚mule⬚.

   (d)   Schools have ⬚pollute⬚ ⬚rules⬚ for
         everyone.

   (e)   Cars ⬚prune⬚ ⬚pollute⬚ the air.

3. Unjumble these **u–e** words.

   (a)   lruse   _____
   (b)   tlpueol   _____

   (c)   etful   _____
   (d)   ubce   _____

   (e)   duer   _____
   (f)   nJeu   _____

   (g)   tuce   _____
   (h)   umel   _____

4. Cover the sheet and see how many **u–e** words you can write here.

   _____

   _____

u–e as in flute

1. Find the answers to these clues.

    (a) An animal like a donkey.   _____

    (b) A piece of ice.   _____

    (c) The 6th month.   _____

    (d) This comes out of a piano.   _____

    (e) Schools have these.   _____

    (f) A musical instrument.   _____

2. Add the missing **u–e** sound to these to make words.
   Draw a picture to show their meanings.

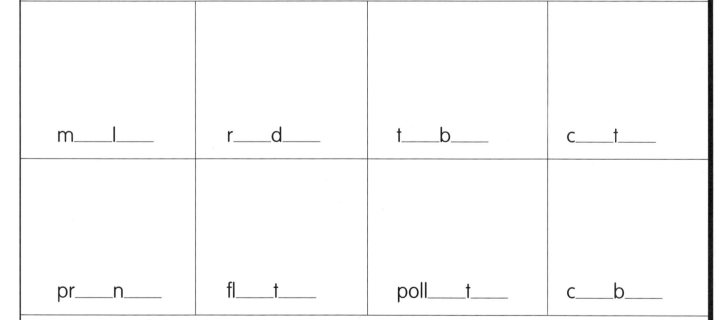

m___l___	r___d___	t___b___	c___t___
pr___n___	fl___t___	poll___t___	c___b___

3. Join the sentence beginning to its correct ending.

    (a) The man played   •   • like cubes.

    (b) Dice are shaped   •   • used the gate.

    (c) A factory can   •   • a tune on the piano.

    (d) The cute mule   •   • pollute the air.

Answers

Page 9   a–e
1. Teacher check
2. Teacher check

Page 10   a–e
1. (a) lake   (b) rake
   (c) tame   (d) male
   (e) mane
2. (a) Teacher check
   (b) Teacher check
   (c) pale

Page 11   ai
1. (a) Teacher check
   (b) train, rain, nail, first
     aid, pail, sail, snail,
     mail, tail
2. (a) tail
   (b) sail; first aid
   (c) mail
   (d) rain
   (e) snail; pail
   (f) nail

Page 12   ai
1. (a) no   (b) no
   (c) no   (d) no
   (e) yes
2. Teacher check
3. (a) The sailing boat sailed
     on the lake.
   (b) A cat's tail is very hairy.
   (c) Snails come out when
     it rains.
   (d) I put the nails in the
     nail pail.
   (e) A train goes on train
     tracks.

Page 13   ey
1. Teacher check
2. (a) prey   (b) whey
   (c) obey   (d) they
3. (a) prey   (b) survey
   (c) they   (d) obey
   (e) hey
4. Teacher check

Page 14   ey
1. (a) A cute bunny is prey to
     a fox.
   (b) Miss Muffet ate curds
     and whey.
2. Teacher check
3. hey, obey, survey, whey,
   they, prey
4. Teacher check

Page 15   ay
1. Teacher check
2. (a) today   (b) hay
   (c) play   (d) stay
   (e) lay
3. Teacher check

Page 16   ay
1. Teacher check
2. (a) pay   (b) today
   (c) hay   (d) crayon
   (e) stay   (f) bay
   (g) tray   (h) may
3. stay, today, play, tray, say
4. Teacher check

Page 17   e
1. Teacher check
2. (a) he   (b) she
   (c) we   (d) me
   (e) evening
3. evening, me, be, he, she,
   even, we
4. Teacher check

Page 18   ea
1. Teacher check
2. teach, beak, flea, clean,
   speak, tea, beat, meat,
   read
3. Teacher check
4. (a) beach
   (b) clean; neat
   (c) eat; meat
   (d) leaf

Page 19   ea
1. Teacher check
2. (a) teach – beach
   (b) bean – clean
   (c) beat – seat
3. Teacher check

Page 20   ee
1. Teacher check
2. (a) feed
   (b) tree; green
   (c) feet; creek
   (d) sheep   (e) bee
3. sheep, sleep, peep, tree,
   feet, bee
4. Teacher check

Page 21   ee
1. Teacher check
2. Teacher check
3. (a) yes   (b) no
   (c) no   (d) yes
   (e) no   (f) yes

Page 22   ey
1. Teacher check
2. (a) jockey   (b) trolley
   (c) honey   (d) monkey
   (e) turkey
3. (a) key   (b) turkey
   (c) donkey   (d) honey
   (e) monkey   (f) parsley
   (g) valley   (h) jockey
4. Teacher check

Page 23   ey
1. (a) yes   (b) no
   (c) no   (d) yes
   (e) yes   (f) no
2. Teacher check
3. monkey, honey, jockey,
   parsley, turkey, valley,
   chimney, trolley

Page 24   ie
1. Teacher check
2. (a) The thief stole the
     team's shield.
   (b) The team showed grief
     for their stolen shield.
   (c) The Indian chief set up
     camp in the field.
   (d) We had a piece of
     cake for supper last
     night.
   (e) I believe that it will rain
     tomorrow.
3. thief, brief, piece, grief,
   chief, field, shield
4. Teacher check

Page 25   ie
1. (a) yes   (b) no
   (c) yes   (d) yes
   (e) no
2. Teacher check
3. (a) thief   (b) shield
   (c) piece   (d) relief
4. Teacher check

Page 26   y
1. Teacher check
2. (a) funny; silly
   (b) puppy; bunny
   (c) jelly
   (d) granny; sorry
3. (a) yes   (b) yes
   (c) no   (d) no
   (e) yes   (f) yes

Page 27   y
1. (a) Mother put a red
     cherry in the jelly.
   (b) My granny was so
     sorry that she made
     me hurry.
   (c) The puppy ate his
     dinner then he ran
     after my bunny.
   (d) When I was sick I felt
     dizzy and my red face
     felt funny.
   (e) Lots of very happy
     people live in the
     green valley.
2. Teacher check
3. (a) happy   (b) funny
   (c) jelly   (d) puppy
   (e) hurry   (f) dizzy
4. (a) funny   (b) granny
   (c) happy   (d) bunny
   (e) cherry

Page 28   i
1. Teacher check
2. (a) kind; iron
   (b) blinds; Friday
   (c) find; tiger
   (d) Behind; spider
3. (a) no   (b) no
   (c) yes   (d) no
   (e) yes   (f) yes
4. Teacher check

Page 29   i
1. Teacher check
2. Teacher check

Page 30   i–e
1. Teacher check
2. (a) five   (b) fine
   (c) drives   (d) line
   (e) bite   (f) time
   (g) hide
3. (a) drives   (b) kite
   (c) bite   (d) time
   (e) fire
4. Teacher check

Page 31   i–e
1. bike, hike, Mike, spike
2. dive, five, hive, live
3. (a) mice   (b) line
   (c) bike   (d) rice
   (e) hive
4. (a) kite   (b) mice
   (c) hike   (d) like
   (e) five   (f) bike
5. Teacher check

Answers

Page 32 — y
1. Teacher check
2. (a) cry (b) fry
   (c) sty (d) shy
   (e) dry (f) why
   (g) fly (h) sky
3. Teacher check
4. Teacher check

Page 33 — o
1. Teacher check
2. (a) A pony ate most of the clover.
   (b) Both of the boys got over the fence.
   (c) The boat had a cargo of fence posts.
   (d) If the gate is open the pony will get away.
3. Teacher check
4. Teacher check

Page 34 — o
1. (a) no (b) yes
   (c) no (d) yes
   (e) yes
2. cargo, pony, total, clover, over, open, most, post, both
3. Teacher check

Page 35 — oa
1. Teacher check
2. (a) yes (b) no
   (c) yes (d) yes
   (e) no
3. coach, boat, roast, toad, coat, soap, toast, road
4. Teacher check

Page 36 — oa
1. (a) coat (b) float
   (c) soap (d) goat
   (e) foam (f) toad
   (g) loaf (h) load
   (i) toast
2. Teacher check
3. Teacher check

Page 37 — o–e
1. Teacher check
2. Teacher check
3. (a) rose (b) bone
   (c) home (d) slope
   (e) nose

Page 38 — o–e
1. Teacher check
2. Teacher check
3. (a) cone (b) home
   (c) stone (d) poke
   (e) bone (f) slope
4. Teacher check

Page 39 — ow
1. Teacher check
2. (a) The big black crow had a yellow beak.
   (b) The hollow in the tree was very narrow.
   (c) I saw a snail in the garden moving very slowly.
   (d) A rabbit lives in a burrow below the ground.
   (e) I will show you how to make my shadow grow.
3. Teacher check

Page 40 — ow
1. (a) shadow
   (b) yellow; hollow
   (c) burrow
   (d) narrow
   (e) grow; slowly
2. (a) hollow (b) slow
   (c) below (d) narrow
   (e) grow (f) crow
3. Teacher check

Page 41 — ew
1. Teacher check
2. (a) blew (b) stew
   (c) crew (d) grew
   (e) threw (f) brew
   (g) jewel (h) chew
3. Teacher check
4. threw, jewel, new, chew, grew, few, blew, crew, stew

Page 42 — ew
1. Teacher check
2. (a) The ship's crew had stew for dinner.
   (b) The wind blew a few leaves off the tree.
   (c) When her feet grew she got new shoes.
   (d) The thief threw the jewel in a new bag.
3. Teacher check

Page 43 — oo
1. Teacher check
2. (a) broom (b) moo
   (c) spoon (d) moon
   (e) boots
3. Teacher check
4. Teacher check

Page 44 — oo
1. (a) yes (b) no
   (c) no (d) yes
   (e) yes
2. Teacher check
3. (a) spoon (b) moon
   (c) boot (d) balloon

Page 45 — u–e
1. Teacher check
2. (a) tune; flute
   (b) use; tube
   (c) rude; prune
   (d) rules (e) pollute
3. (a) rules (b) pollute
   (c) flute (d) cube
   (e) rude (f) June
   (g) cute (h) mule
4. Teacher check

Page 46 — u–e
1. (a) mule (b) cube
   (c) June (d) tune
   (e) rules (f) flute
2. Teacher check
3. (a) The man played a tune on the piano.
   (b) Dice are shaped like a cube.
   (c) A factory can pollute the air.
   (d) The cute mule used the gate.